THE ALLEGATIONS AGA[INST D. ROBERT] WHITE...

"If I happened to be a law[yer, I] would try to put D. Robert W[hite in jail and otherwise] curtail his liberties. He has given away all the trade secrets of the legal dodge.... May this good and funny man live forever."

—Larry L. King,
author of *The Best Little Whorehouse in Texas*

"The question is whether D. Robert White will be banned by the rest of the profession."

—UPI Radio

"Guilty of humorous writing."   —*Atlanta Constitution*

...AND *WHITE'S LAW DICTIONARY*

"D. Robert White's legal advice and politicians' promises have a common thread: Caveat emptor!"

—U.S. Senator Birch Bayh

"When the next judge throws the book at one of my clients, I hope it's this book. It would make great jail-house reading."

—Professor Alan M. Dershowitz,
Harvard Law School

"Law students around the country should read WHITE'S LAW DICTIONARY, if for no other reason than to note the levels to which legal scholarship has descended."

—Professor Charles Alan Wright
University of Texas
Co-Author, Wright & Miller,
Federal Practice and Procedure

"At last, a book that gives us a fighting chance at understanding what lawyers mean when they say something—even if they don't mean it when they say it."

—Jim Fisk and Robert Barron
BUZZWORDS—The Official MBA Dictionary

WHITE'S
LAW
DICTIONARY

D. Robert White, Esq.

Illustrated by Mike Goodman

WARNER BOOKS

A Warner Communications Company

Warner Books, Inc., 666 Fifth Avenue, New York, NY 10103

 A Warner Communications Company

Printed in the United States of America
First Printing: December 1985
10 9 8 7 6 5 4 3 2 1

Designed by Giorgetta Bell McRee

Library of Congress Cataloging in Publication Data

White, D. Robert (Daniel Robert)
  White's Law dictionary.

  1. Law—United States—Dictionaries—Anecdotes,
facetiae, satire, etc. I. Title. II. Title: dictionary.
K184.W46   1985   340′.03′21   85-11502
ISBN 0-446-38259-0 (U.S.A.) (pbk.)
      0-446-38260-4 (Canada) (pbk.)

I dedicate this book with gratitude
to my professors at the
Columbia Law School

ACKNOWLEDGMENTS

I wish especially to thank Martin J. Yudkowitz, my law school classmate, moot-court partner, and collaborator (although not my lawyer). Also: David Wescoe, whose material I have been using without attribution since our first year at Columbia Law School; the lovely, lawyerly Lisa Robertson, an inspiration on many levels; Randy Turk, whom I want on my side if I ever go into court (or a singles' bar); Dale "Big Guy" Adler, who appreciates lawyers as only a physician can; Nancy Feins, whose unpulled punches helped sort the wheat from the chaff; Mat Epstein, who helped restore the chaff to the wheat; Paul Glist, my former colleague and one of lawyerdom's great closet humorists; John Fleming and John Bonds, two lawyers whose wit has miraculously survived partnership in a prestigious Atlanta law firm; and Bob Steed, a similarly successful lawyer whose wit has survived a municipal bond practice—even more miraculous.

I would also thank John Freund and David Porter, literary entrepreneurs who started the ball rolling; Helen Rees, my resourceful agent; and David Vigliano and Claire Zion, my able editors at Warner Books.

The Generosity to Aspiring Writers Award is hereby offered to Larry L. King.

It was, as always, a pleasure to work with Mike Goodman, whose wonderful cartoons grace this volume.

TWO INTRODUCTORY NOTES

To Lawyers

What does it take to be a great lawyer?

A precise analytical mind? Two dozen charcoal-gray suits with vests? A foxy secretary named Della, a handsome private eye named Drake, and a criminal populace prone to public confession?

On a recent national television program, columnist George Will asked the famous California trial lawyer Melvin Belli about lawyers' compensation. Will questioned the propriety of contingent fees—fees based on a percentage of funds recovered (e.g., 30 percent of a $1 million verdict)—in situations where a large recovery is certain. The usual justification for giving the lawyer a percentage rather than an hourly rate is that it's his reward for taking the risk of no recovery at all. But sometimes, as in cases concerning a downed plane, even the worst lawyer couldn't avoid a whopping judgment if he ran from it.

Will's question was a hard one, to which there's no real answer—other than that if there were more cushy television commentator positions available, maybe lawyers wouldn't be lawyers at all. I personally would have commenced tapping my earphone (it was a long-distance interview) and pretended to be getting no sound.

But Melvin Belli, a lawyer's lawyer, rose to the challenge, demonstrating in the process his polished trial lawyer's capacity for thinking on his feet, even when he's sitting down. Before a lesser lawyer could have uttered a single "anything herein to the contrary notwithstanding," Melvin had delivered his unanswerable riposte: "It's a *res ipsa loquitur* kind of thing."

And it was done!

His delivery was masterful, his Latin pronunciation sublime. No voice at a burning bush ever sounded more authoritative. It brought to mind Churchill's description of premodern war: "cruel but magnificent." Belli's interrogator, like a wounded bull, snorted and pawed the ground, but the spectators knew the fight was over. Only bigness of heart prevented Melvin from going in over the horns for the fatal thrust.

There's an important lesson in this story. Somewhere.

Belli's Latin phrase translates: "The thing (*res*) speaks (*loquitur*) for itself (*ipsa*)." Note that the words are out of order. (As an historical aside, this word order problem appears to have originated sometime after the death of Julius Caesar, whose "*Et tu, Brute*" ["And you, Brutus"] was just fine. Caesar's influence on grammatical and other public matters was on the wane at the time.)

What, you ask, does "*res ipsa loquitur*" have to do with contingent fees? *Exactly!* Nothing! Zilch. Diddlysquat (which itself is a term Belli might have employed with equal logic, if not equal appearance of erudition). A confidently propounded piece of jargon stands on its own authority, immune from normal requirements of relevance (not to mention good taste). It marks its source as a person whose views deserve deference if not, *ipso facto*, indeed, abject groveling self-abasement.

And that's what this dictionary is all about.

The essence of lawyerdom, of commanding proper respect for your opinions, however groundless, is *sounding* like a lawyer. That, in turn, requires the proper vocabulary—a wellspring of terms whose mere utterance, *at random*, can cloud any conversation, divert any discussion, avoid any answer. Melvin Belli obviously understood this. So did Abraham Lincoln, whose ability to obfuscate something as straightforward as a number—"Four score and seven years ago" —had people eating out of his hand.

Remember: Confusion conveys control.

This brings us to the question of how extensive your arsenal needs to be. Lawyers say words are their stock in trade. If so, they are burdened by an excess of inventory. Consider a volume which by default has held primacy among legal lexicons since its original publication in 1891: *Black's Law Dictionary*.

The preface to *Black's* states that the latest edition includes 10,000 entries. Let's examine some of those 10,000.

A random perusal turns up *zemindar*. You think, "Wow, I really didn't know that one. Good thing I have *Black's*." Its definition? "In Hindu law, landkeeper." You sigh a breath of relief; thank God your ignorance of zemindars didn't come up in public.

Flipping back to the beginning, you see:

A The first letter in the English and most other alphabets derived from the Roman or Latin alphabet, which was one of several ancient Italian alphabets derived from the Greek, which was an adaptation of the Phoenician.

Amazing. Just the other day you were wondering if that wasn't adapted from the Phoenician.

Come on, Mr. Black, what gives?

Do we really need a sixty-seven-word definition of "wrongful act," including a citation to a decision of the Illinois Court of Appeals? You couldn't leave it at "something one shouldn't do"?

How about "*Apt* Fit; suitable; appropriate"? Do I see a little padding to get the total up to 10,000?

And "*Cerebellum* Lower portion of brain below back of cerebrum concerned with muscular coordination and body equilibrium"—aren't we poaching a wee bit on another profession's turf?

My own dictionary has somewhat fewer than 10,000 definitions. Call me slapdash—I overlooked *zemindar*. But it contains, I submit, more than enough jargon to enable you to drape a cloak of darkness over whatever subject you're addressing.

Every term you could ever use in your legal career? Not quite, briefcase-breath. But enough.

And it's small enough to be carried to parties and on dates.

A few legal greenhorns out there may ask, "Why do we need *any* dictionary, portable or otherwise? What is Continuing Legal Education for, if not constantly to feed us new terms that laymen haven't yet figured out?"

Have you looked at those CLE courses lately? The catalogue for the most recent major bar convention lists: Environmental Law (protecting the moose); Food and Drug Law (protecting the mousse); Copyright Law (protecting the muse); Commodities Law (protecting the maize); Sports Law (protecting the Mays); Antivivisection Law (protecting the mice); Criminal Law for Public Officials (protecting the Meese); Communications Law (protecting the Morse); Family Law (protecting the Ms.); Labor Law (protecting Lamaze).

Somebody in the CLE office is yanking your chain.

Law review credentials, Supreme Court certificates, a secretary who'll proofread—those things are nice, but dispensable. Like a cummerbund. This dictionary is basic.

Even if it weren't, it's available now, and you can't afford to be the only one around without it. You're not being paranoid when you suspect people are gunning for you—it's a cutthroat world. This book is your sword and your shield. Don't leave home without it.

To Laymen

Ours is a jargon-ridden society. Physicians at cocktail parties drop terms like "thrombolysis," "angioplasty," and "croak." Dentists at polo games discuss "bicuspids," "periodontalism," and "portfolio management." Accountants would undoubtedly be just as bad if they ever got invited out.

Social psychologists say that such specialized language serves an "intra-group recognition function"—which proves they do it, too.

So why do people curse and fume so much harder when they encounter it in lawyers?

Who knows?

It may be because people don't *like* lawyers—which admittedly just recasts the question. But it's important that we get this out in the open.

It wasn't always this way. In fact, it wasn't always the way it was before it became the way it is now. Which isn't to say that the way it was before it became the way it was before the way it is now is the same as the way it is now. However, there are similarities.

Not twenty years ago (not eighteen years ago, either; it was more like nineteen years), lawyers were perceived as okay people. You didn't want your daughter marrying one, but pogroms against lawyers were infrequent.

Back then, if you asked somebody whose names came to mind when he thought about lawyers, he might well have said (you can play this game yourself—pick three names)...Abraham Lincoln, Clarence Darrow, and Perry Mason—decent people all. If he had picked E. G. Marshall of *The Defenders* instead of Perry Mason, the final package would have been essentially the same.

Of course, someone who associated the legal profession with two dead people and a television character arguably wasn't right on top of things in the field. But the point stands.

Seeds of change were sown in the late sixties, when the country seemed to be falling apart. Eyes turned to Washington, to see who was screwing things up, and lawyers were found infesting the place. Actually, for a while, lawyers were able to lay low, letting the military-industrial complex take the heat. But then the Watergate hearings blew the cover.

Even as public scrutiny of the profession increased, familiarity breeding contempt, the ranks of law schools burgeoned; the baby-boom generation finally realized it had to get a job.

A lot of these baby-boomers weren't meant for the law. They should have gone for Ph.D.s in art, music, or some other harmless field. A few did go for Ph.D.s but got tired of driving cabs. One way or another, 93.4 percent of them ended up in the law.

How, you might well ask, did they all get into something as

competitive as law school? This country currently boasts 174 American Bar Association–approved law schools (175 if you count the U.S. Army Judge Advocate General's School, which I don't); every literate primate in the country could get in *some*where.

To say these baby-boomers weren't meant for the law is definitely not to say they weren't meant for law *school*. They were—and are— natural students: bright, fun-loving, averse to shaving, adept with a Frisbee. But in private practice they found themselves round pegs in square holes, free spirits in an army of conformists, tennis shoes in a closet full of wingtips.

It's not hard to sympathize with their plight. Nobody describes what lawyers do as *fun*:

> Hello, Liz? Dave. Yeah, listen, I know we talked about seeing that new play at Lincoln Center, but I was wondering if you wouldn't like to come over and curl up with a bottle of Beaujolais and some good mortgage documents....No, not mine.... Oh, I'm glad you liked those, and we could definitely reread them sometime. What I had in mind was, this new guy has moved in next door, practices at Sullivan & Cromwell, and he says his are really long and complicated....Yeah, tons of Latin....And he'd be willing to lend them to us for an evening....

In the words of the New York jurisprudential philosopher Martin J. Yudkowitz, "The law is not pretty."

What's my point? That lawyers are in fact great guys? Let's not go overboard.

I'm saying have a heart. There but for the grace of God goes your dog. It's not as if lawyers *enjoy* being the way they are, and in any event, they're no worse than doctors. They may even be a little better—when was the last time someone at your *lawyer's* office ordered you to take off all your clothes and then left you sitting naked in a cold room for an hour?

Admittedly, none of the foregoing solves the problem of how to deal with lawyers and their jargon. Indeed, is this concern for the plight of lawyers not a case of the tail wagging the dog? Six hundred fifty thousand lawyers in one country might sound like a lot, particularly since five or six are enough to kill even a big party (the way even one deceased rodent in your beer mug can kill your thirst), but what about the remaining 200 million laymen in the country?

No one familiar with these statistics would dispute that there's a serious shortage of lawyers in this country. The sorry truth is, literally thousands of Americans can't have their own lawyer, but must share one—which is not only unjust, but unsanitary.

But the original questions remains: how to deal with the lawyers we already have. What is a layman to do?

Enter this legal lexicon.

If you master but a fraction of its defined terms, which number slightly shy of 10,000, wondrous changes in your life will ensue.

No more will you have to hang back, stupidly suspecting you've been insulted when a lawyer at the club locker room characterizes you as "obviously a person of few codicils." No more will you have to spend long hours at the end of social functions searching for your date or spouse, only to find her (or him) in a crowd of admirers surrounding...a lawyer, propounding a polysyllabic perspective on life.

This book won't make you a lawyer—but it might make people *think* you're a lawyer. And with that warning, you're on your own.

D.R.W., *1985*

WHITE'S LAW DICTIONARY

ABA *A*merican *B*ar *A*ssociation, a social club dedicated to the tax-deductible enjoyment of major American cities and resorts. Also known as American Boondoggle Association.

ab initio Latin, "from the outset." Refers to the moment in your conversation with your lawyer when his billing meter begins to run.

accord and satisfaction **1:** discharge of a contract-based claim, whereby the original terms of the contract are altered to accord greater satisfaction to one of the parties.
2: lascivious indulgence in the backseat of a small Japanese automobile.

action lawsuit. A term used by lawyers to distract the client from the fact that nothing is happening in his case.

act of God in the law of contracts, a term used to describe any natural event—such as a flood, earthquake, or revolution—that occurs without fault on the part of either party but the costs of which one of the parties must bear. In large law

ABA CONVENTION

firms, also known as "act of name partner."

ad damnum   Latin, "to the damage." **1:** the clause in a complaint which states the amount of money claimed in the lawsuit.

2: a common legal exclamation, especially in the southern United States.

ad hominem   Latin, "to the person." An argument addressed not to the legal issues of a case but to the parties involved—or their parents, *e.g.,* "Yo' momma."

administrative expertise   the mythical expertise of administrative agencies, to which judges claim to defer when reviewing agency orders and regulations that are too long and boring to bother reading.

adultery   the crime of having more fun than society considers it seemly for an adult to have.

adverse possession   also known as "squatters' rights," this is the ultimate way to acquire real estate with "no money down." It involves simply pitching tent on a piece of land and not moving for twenty years, not even to go to the bathroom. The cases say your use of the land must be "open," "exclusive," and "continuous"—the way certain bohemians have gained legal title to Washington, D.C., subway vents, and the way the DuPonts took over Delaware.

affidavit   a client's sworn statement of whatever facts his lawyer believes necessary to win the case.

affirmance   A determination by an appellate court that a ruling of the trial court is correct (i.e., too complex for review).

AD DAMNUM

"Ad damnum." "Ad nauseum."

affirmative action **1:** as originally conceived, the preferential hiring of minorities and women.
2: under the Reagan administration, hiring *anybody*.

a fortiori Latin, "for a still stronger reason." A term used by lawyers to link an indisputable premise to an inexplicable conclusion.

allegation a purportedly factual statement pertaining to a lawsuit. *See* allegory; fable.

AMA *A*merican *M*edical *A*ssociation, an investment club specializing in the purchase of swampland. Lawyers have mixed feelings toward this rival professional organization, partly because doctors get special license plates, but mainly because there are no professional basketball players called "Lawyer J." The ambivalence lawyers feel toward doctors can be summed up in the question, "If they're so stupid, how come they have all the money?"

ambulance chasing what personal injury lawyers refer to as "client development."

American lawyer **1:** a term of contempt employed by foreigners for particularly noisy (and noisome) tourists.
2: a monthly tabloid that aspires to do for the legal profession what Upton Sinclair's *The Jungle* did for the meat-packing industry.

amicus curiae Latin, "friend of the court." Someone who is permitted to submit arguments to a court which the actual parties to the pending dispute would not dare submit. (These arguments are met with the same warm appreciation

AMBULANCE CHASING

"This one's yours, Covington. . . . Go get 'em!"

you feel for the unsolicited opinions of a by-stander to your marital dispute in a crowded department store.)

annual report a corporation's yearly report card to its shareholders. A richly imaginative document similar to the report cards the company's officers had to take home to their parents during grade school, except now there are no teachers around to spoil their fun by making them tell the truth.

antenuptial contract a "before the wedding" contract, usually utilized by a wealthy person to limit the portion of his or her fortune that a prospective spouse could obtain in a divorce. A triumph of experience over hope.

appointment book the reference of last resort when trying to duck undesired invitations ("Darn it, I seem to be scheduled for depositions through 1988") or when trying to figure out what the hell you did this past year ("I only billed four hundred hours?").

arbitrator a term used by the disgruntled parties on both sides of a dispute to describe the "independent" negotiator who sold each of them down the river. Derived from a combination of *arbitrary* and *traitor.*

arguendo Latin, "for the sake of argument." A term used by lawyers to suggest that their client should win, even assuming the client actually did what the other side's 147 eyewitnesses saw him do. Not to be confused with *innuendo,* a popular Italian suppository.

AMICUS CURIAE

arrest the detention of someone presumed by a policeman to be guilty, for the sake of conferring upon him a presumption of innocence.

ASAP *As Soon As Possible.* **1:** an implied term of any work request from a senior lawyer to a junior lawyer, the term "possible" carrying no qualifications, such as "allowing for food and sleep."
2: a label placed on urgent interoffice notes, generally translated by the receiving secretary to mean *Ask Someone After Payday.*

as is with regard to sales of goods, a term that negates the existence of warranties, express or implied. If you purchase a pig "as is," it might or might not grunt. If you accept a date with a football player as is, he might or might not have a neck (although he will certainly grunt). Ronald Reagan ran for the presidency "as is."

assault a threat by one individual to make harmful or offensive contact with another, accompanied by a present apparent ability to carry out that threat. Fear engendered in the threatened party is the essence of this tort, in contrast to *battery,* which requires that actual contact be made. Thus, if you spit at someone and miss, but he saw you aiming, that's *assault* (except at punk-rock discos, where it's considered an erotic come-on). If you spit at someone and hit, but he never saw it coming, that's *battery.* If you spit at someone and hit, and he saw you aiming but was too slow to dodge, that's *assault and battery.* (And if you just ate a tuna fish sandwich with onions, that's *assault with a deadly weapon.*)

assertion a statement without support or reason; in particular, any argument put forth by your opposing counsel. Especially strong arguments by opposing counsel are known as *bald* assertions.

associate a usually young member of a law firm who does not have a vote in the firm's decisions and whose compensation package consists not of a percentage of firm profits but of a fixed salary, along with such perks as twenty-four-hour access to the firm's library. Derives from "ass," as in (a) beast of burden, and (b) sucker or fool.

assumption **1:** in the law of contracts, an agreement by an outside party to step into the shoes of one of the original parties to a contract and "assume" that original party's contractual obligations.
2: in business, a premise used to construct annual budgets and marketing forecasts when you are too lazy to do the research.

assumption of risk in the law of torts, a legal defense based on the theory that the plaintiff must have *known*—and hence voluntarily took his chances—that hockey pucks fly into the stands, that nitro-burning "funny cars" run off the track and burst into flames, or that Amtrak passengers have a 60 percent chance of survival.

automated office the office of the future, where your secretary will be replaced with a word processor, an electronic mailbox, and a robotics system capable of ordering your spouse an anniversary present and bending over when it reaches into file cabinets.

ASSOCIATE

"Aren't you glad you're not sitting on some hot gritty beach sipping piña coladas and surrounded by half-naked beach bunnies who wouldn't know a trust indenture from a codicil?"

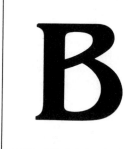

bail   money or other property given to ensure
that a person released from custody will return
at an appointed time. The amount of bail is an
arbitrary figure reflecting a judge's determination of the detainee's risk to society, his likeli-
hood of appearing at the appointed time, his
racial resemblance to the judge, and the likeli-
hood that his friends and family know where
the judge lives.

bailee   **1:** in the law of contracts, one to whom
goods are entrusted or "bailed."
2: in the law of admiralty, a person who by
virtue of high age or low IQ may lawfully be
ejected from an imperiled ship, with or without
formal ceremonies.

bankruptcy   life after debt.

bar exam   a two- to three-day examination given
twice each year around the county and required
for the practice of law by everyone but accountants, lobbyists, summer law clerks, real estate
agents, *pro se* litigants, law professors, paralegals,

THE BAR

"I think you'll like this place, McDermott. It's stuffy and pretentious."

legal secretaries, members of Congress, and some judges.

belts and suspenders refers to provisions in legal documents that are duplicative or redundant, just as belts and suspenders are sartorially redundant on all but the most interesting physiques.

bench warrant a guaranteed seat in court.

battle of the bladder a high-risk game of chicken used during down-to-the-wire labor negotiations, when (having consumed many cups of coffee) both sides agree not to leave the room until they reach a settlement.

bigamy double jeopardy.

billable hours a fictional number employed by lawyers in billing clients. This figure includes time spent jogging, eating, getting to work, flirting with the client's receptionist, and calculating this figure. The ratio of billable hours to hours actually worked is approximately three to one. For legal associates in New York, the ratio of billable hours to hours in a month is approximately one to one.

Black's Law Dictionary an overlarge medieval legal lexicon. Preeminent in the field, until recently.

Blue Book the informal name of a pamphlet—infrequently blue, never a book—formally entitled *A Uniform System of Citation*. Revered as the Bible, Koran, Talmud, Upanishad, and *Harvard Law Review* of legal citation, the Blue Book is updated every four years by the law review editors of Harvard, Columbia, Yale, and the University of Pennsylvania, the students at these schools having exhibited a sufficient level of anality, as well as a bizarre urge to immortalize their names in the illustrative case citations.

blue-collar crime any of various tacky crimes committed by untutored individuals with absolutely no sense of decorum—or of where the big money is. *Compare* white-collar crime.

blue sky laws a crazy quilt of state securities laws enacted to prevent snake-oil salesmen from selling John Q. Public "the blue sky." Because similar federal laws cover much of the same turf, these are often cited as an example of unnecessary regulation—especially in Los Angeles, where the last verified sighting of blue sky was in 1963.

board of directors a group elected by shareholders to protect management's interests. Being a director of a major company is a great honor, and those who qualify consider it their obligation to do double, triple, and even quadruple duty; at last count the boards of the Fortune 500 companies consisted of only 193 individuals—192 if you don't count Mikhail Gorbachev as being on the board of Occidental Petroleum.

boilerplate any standard language—from a single clause to numerous pages—used in identical form in a large number of legal documents, the client being charged for each document as if composed from scratch.

brain death **1:** in criminal law, one of various tests for determining whether an assault victim has died (even though breathing and other vital

BOARD OF DIRECTORS

"The good news is, the directors will be participating in the company's record profits this quarter. The bad news is, the shareholders will not."

BRAIN DEATH

"...heh, heh, that was one great case, let me tell you. 'Course, not as great as the one I argued before the same judge in 1957..."

functions may continue) and hence whether the assailant should be tried for homicide or instead some lesser offense.

2: a test, proposed but never enacted, for determining the continuing eligibility for office of elderly judges and some U.S. presidents.

3: a near certain consequence of prolonged exposure to the Code of Federal Regulations.

branch office an imperialist outpost in a legal hinterland (e.g., Washington, D.C.) established to plunder the local environs for the benefit of the home office. Occasionally staffed by recalcitrant natives dangerously prone to asserting their independence.

Brandeis brief any unusually lengthy brief—often containing graphs, charts, and endless sociological data—similar to those produced by Louis D. Brandeis, the brilliant jurist whose mammoth tomes gave new meaning to "the weight of authority."

brief a document containing legal arguments and designed to persuade a judge to rule in one's favor. To the extent that the term suggests brevity, it constitutes the only monosyllabic oxymoron in the English language.

briefcase a leather lunch pail. A "power accessory" that marks the carrier as an important decision-maker, even if the only thing it contains is a bologna sandwich, and the carrier's only decision-making authority is setting the darkness control on the office copying machine.

BRANDEIS BRIEFS

"I don't care what the Brethren say, Louis. I say they look stupid."

camel's nose a figurative term referring to something that lawyers profess an urgent desire to keep out of "the tent." A lawyer will frequently argue that to permit obvious justice to prevail against his client's interest in *this* case would establish a precedent by which later courts might work injustice. Thus, to allow the camel's nose inside the tent runs the risk that the unthinking beast will carry away the entire structure (or take up residence there), just as an unthinking legal system might deprive a lawyer of the edifice of Middle Eastern metaphorical malarky beneath which his client's misdeeds seek shelter.

capital gains tax accrual and unusual form of capital punishment.

capital punishment 1: death by electrocution, lethal injection, asphyxiation, or any other method likely to achieve the desired behavior modification of hardened criminals. Applied only to murderers and, in Texas, people who write bad checks. Its rehabilitative value was established centuries ago by the English prisoner who commented as he approached the gallows, "This will certainly teach me a lesson."

2: in Washington, D.C., a form of severe punishment consisting of requiring the offender to listen to several days' worth of congressional speeches (or, alternatively, oral arguments before the U.S. Tax Court). This is now considered too brutal no matter what the crime.

casebook an encyclopedia-sized volume for the instruction of law students and the enrichment of law professors. Consists primarily of the republication of judicial opinions and other materials already in the public domain, for which no royalties need be paid.

case method the traditional method of legal instruction, focusing on actual decided cases rather than statutes and rules of law. Preferable because it requires use of a *casebook* (see above).

certiorari **1:** a breath mint popular among Italian-American trial lawyers.

2: a writ, or order, by which the U.S. Supreme Court indicates its willingness to review, or "certify," rulings of lower courts. The process of granting or denying certiorari is precise and highly predictable, notwithstanding reports that the High Court's closed-door certiorari conferences are accompanied by shouts of "Heads!" and "Tails!"

Christmas an annual occasion once thought to have religious overtones but which the Burger Court has now declared to be purely "cultural"

CERTIORARI

"Tails! Cert. denied."

(the rationale for its ruling that cities may spend public funds on traditional manger scenes). The Court was understandably influenced by that pagan ritual known as the "office Christmas party," which traditionally features activities that have little to do with religion and that in fact bear a striking resemblance to fertility rites dating back to well before Christ.

churning with reference to unnecessary purchases and sales of stocks, a sin of commission.

civil procedure proceduralized incivility.

class action a lawsuit with a large number of "similarly situated" people on one side or the other. E.g., a suit against Colgate-Palmolive on behalf of Ultra-Brite users who never scored; a suit against ABC on behalf of viewers of "20/20" who came down with lockjaw after prolonged exposure to Barbara Walters; or a suit on behalf of purchasers of Raid who still have roaches the size of hamsters.

client someone whose aversion to the other party in a lawsuit or distrust of the other side in a deal exceeds his aversion to lawyers. Also known as "meal ticket," "gravy train," and "pigeon."

client development the label applied by lawyers to tax-deductible, three-martini lunches with their golfing buddies.

commodity any undifferentiated product, such as wheat, pork bellies, Johnny Carson reruns, Barry Manilow albums, and recent law-school graduates.

common pleas **1:** the title of certain courts of

COMMODITY

"It's a pleasure to welcome you free-thinking, ruggedly independent young lawyers to Quibble & Quiver."

limited jurisdiction in medieval England and modern Pennsylvania.

2: any of various undignified forms of begging by lawyers for the performance of conjugal rituals with their uninspired spouses. (E.g., "Please, dear, my briefs are overdue.")

common stock 1: a certificate representing ownership of a portion of a corporation, each share usually carrying voting rights but no guaranteed dividends or priority claims in the event of liquidation of the company.

2: bovine, porcine, or other agricultural creatures prone to vulgar humor and often appearing at black-tie functions with unpolished hooves.

competition in antitrust law, a much-discussed, but little-understood, principle of economic activity stoutly supported by legislators and regulators for all industries except those to which they plan to return at the end of their terms.

concurring opinion a device employed by judges who, in fact, disagree with a ruling but lack the backbone to dissent—or to sit up straight without starch in their robes.

conscience a disease of the brain. Painful for anyone, but fatal for a lawyer. Fortunately, very rare in the profession.

conservator someone legally empowered to hold and manage your assets when you become unable to take care of them yourself. Not greatly different from the role currently envisioned by your spouse.

consortium paradise lost. A polite term for what

people allege the loss of when their spouses are injured or otherwise prevented from performing intimate marital functions.

contingent fee a pay-only-if-you-win fee arrangement whereby your lawyer agrees to handle your case for a percentage of any damages recovered. The percentage is usually three-quarters to nine-tenths of the recovery—if your lawyer is asking less, he's performing an act of charity. A properly appreciative client will let the lawyer have the whole thing, plus a tip (15 percent of the original claim would not be unreasonable).

contract a piece of paper that marries two parties together by explicitly anticipating every eventuality of their divorce. Contracts should always be in writing, as oral contracts aren't worth the paper they're printed on.

contributory negligence **1:** a legal defense based on the theory that the plaintiff's loss was at least partially his own fault.
2: in Manhattan, the doctrine that anyone who leaves a car guarded by fewer than a dozen Dobermans is as much to blame as the person who steals it.

controlled substance a catchall statutory term for marijuana, cocaine, and other drugs seized from unlawful traffickers for use by off-duty policemen.

cop acronym for *c*onstable *o*n *p*atrol. To prosecutors, a martyr whose selfless devotion to the public safety is exceeded only by his unerring memory and his scrupulous respect for the constitutional rights of armed assailants. To defense lawyers, a not-so-latent fascist whose volatility of temper is exceeded only by his limited powers of recall and his penchant for taking target practice in minority neighborhoods.

corner office **1:** an office with windows on two sides, with which a senior partner in a law firm is rewarded during his twilight years for having spent the prime of his life without the vaguest idea of what goes on in the world outside.

2: the generic term for an office where law firms place senior attorneys so old and unpredictable that they need to be watched from all sides.

corpus delicti **1:** Latin, "the body of a crime." The substance or foundation of an unlawful act (e.g., the charred remains of a building, the crushed panel of a car, the mutilated body of anyone but a tow-truck operator).

2: Greek, "delicious corpse." A fastidious brand of cannibalism peculiar to the Canadian provinces and northern Montana.

counterclaim a return volley by a defendant against a plaintiff. Usually a groundless defensive maneuver designed to up the ante in order to force the plaintiff to settle. To paraphrase Sir Isaac Newton, for every lawsuit there is an equal and opposite lawsuit.

CPA *C*ertified *P*ublic *A*ccountant. Although these bean counters are known among business people as *C*onstant *P*ains in the *A*ss, they are beloved by lawyers as the only professionals lawyers can look down on as more boring than

CORNER OFFICE

"Something happens to a lawyer when you put
him in a corner office."

themselves. (CPAs, in turn, look down on actuaries.)

crime against nature a generic statutory term for certain acts, judicially referred to as "icky," that people commit with their pets. Also embraces a number of acts that people, including legislators, commit with each other but that legislators pretend to deem unsavory so people won't inquire too closely into what the legislators are up to with their pages.

curtesy the common-law right of a widower to take possession of all real estate owned by his wife during their marriage. It was as a direct result of, and in compensation for, this legal doctrine that God created more widows than widowers.

CRIME AGAINST NATURE

"How was it for you?"

damnum absque injuria Latin, "loss without injury." A polite reference to the resignation of senior partners.

deadwood anyone in your law firm who is more senior than you are.

deep pocket a client in such serious trouble that his lawyer may charge him for expensive meals, exotic travel, cashmere sweaters, and tropical fish without fear that he will choose to concede guilt rather than pay the bill.

defamation a false communication that tends to subject a person to hatred, contempt, decomposed fruit, or small dead animals. A communication does not constitute defamation if it is an expression of opinion ("I consider Sam to be a loathsome scumsucker") rather than an assertion of fact ("On September 17, I saw Sam on his knees loathsomely sucking scum from his pond").

defendant in civil cases, someone whose net assets are equal to or greater than the cost to someone else of hiring a lawyer.

Delaware a mythical state maintained by the U.S. Postal Service as a forwarding address for two-thirds of the country's largest corporations. In this business utopia, taxes are minimal, local regulations are hospitable to management, and there are more registered corporations than registered voters. Judging from the port of record on the stern of most corporate stinkpots, Delaware is indeed the ultimate "safe harbor."

de minimis Latin, abbreviation of *"De minimis non curat lex,"* or "The law does not care about small things." A doctrine precluding medical malpractice claims by professional athletes alleging brain damage.

Legal Graffiti

There once was a man named Rex,
Whose "thing" was too small for his sex.
He went in for exposure,
The court said, on disclosure,
"De minimis non curat lex."

deposition the taking of testimony from a witness not in open court but under oath and in the presence of a stenographer. Depositions serve various purposes: harassing opposing parties, training junior lawyers, allowing the defending lawyers to take naps with the meter running, and recording the witness's testimony before he forgets or the Mafia informs him they know the route his children take to school.

DEVIL'S ADVOCATE

"The substance of your testimony was fine, but henceforth try to avoid sounding so devil-may-care."

derivative action **1:** a lawsuit filed by a shareholder on behalf of a corporation.

2: with reference to vicarious thrills, the only kind of "action" most lawyers can expect.

dictaphone an office device beloved by lawyers for its inability to fall asleep when spoken to.

discovery **1:** the lengthy and, for the lawyers, lucrative process of obtaining everything but useful information about the opposing party in a lawsuit. (The "good stuff" is routinely withheld on grounds of irrelevance or legal privilege.)

2: a generic term for devices used by defense lawyers to postpone indefinitely the resolution of losing cases.

divorce the legal dissolution of a marriage, involving the division of children among the former spouses—and the division of bank accounts among the lawyers.

diversity suit **1:** a lawsuit in which the jurisdiction of a federal court is based, by statute, on the diversity of the state citizenship of the parties—e.g., the plaintiff (the fellow with the tire tracks on his face) is from Alabama, and the defendant (the fellow who was driving the cement truck) is from Texas.

2: any Doc Severinsen–style sartorial combination—e.g., pinstripe suit, plaid shirt, club tie, argyle socks, and Adidas running shoes—that conspicuously clashes.

dogmeat **1:** what your legal career will amount to if you fail to master this dictionary.

2: what your legal career will amount to if

DICTAPHONE

"Mrs. Philpott, take a letter to the Honorable Durant Carter. . . . Dear Judge Carter, I have now had an opportunity to review your opinion in detail and I must say, in all candor, that it sucks eggs."

DIVERSITY SUIT

you're a lawyer whose name appears in the acknowledgments of this dictionary.

domicile your true home, of which for legal purposes you may have only one, in contrast to your "residence," of which you may have as many as you like, including your chalet in Switzerland, your bungalow in Malibu, your pied-à-terre on Central Park West, and your place in line at the automobile registration window.

double billing a conservative approach to billing, whereby only two clients are billed for a given unit of time, as opposed to the usual three or four. Very rare.

dower **1:** the common-law right of a widow to take possession of one-third of the real estate owned by her husband during their marriage.
2: the expression on a husband's face upon learning that his wife is entitled to the above.

draft **1:** in normal conversation, a first or preliminary writing, subject to revision.
2: in the law, especially as used by senior lawyers demanding work from junior lawyers, a misnomer signifying a polished final product, suitable for framing—or, more to the point, suitable for delivery to the client without additional work by the senior lawyer.

due process **1:** a term that appears in the fifth and fourteenth amendments to the U.S. Constitution, referring to the procedural protections that the sheriff who arrested you and rerouted your intestines with a billy club is required to swear you were accorded.

2: what tabloid newspapers call a "technicality."

dying declaration   a statement admissible in court, notwithstanding its technical status of "hearsay," on the theory that no one lies when he is about to meet his Maker. Reformers are seeking to enact exceptions to the dying declaration rule for politicians, insurance salesmen, and litigators.

egress in real property law, an exit. In general, a way out, which is what every lawyer wants.

ejectment **1:** at common law, a lawsuit to take possession of land and eject persons unlawfully holding or occupying it.

2: the desirable aspect of fee tail (*see*).

electric chair a high-tech device for encouraging compliance with law, especially by minorities.

EIS *E*nvironmental *I*mpact *S*tatement. A lengthy document statutorily required of governmental agencies preparing to take any action likely to have a "significant impact on the environment." Conservatives would deny the need for an EIS prior to filling and paving the Grand Canyon for condominiums; liberals would require an EIS prior to an individual bureaucrat's use of aerosol deodorant or consumption of Mexican food.

escheat the process by which the government takes possession of the property of persons who die without heirs. Derived from the verb *to cheat*.

escrow an agreement between two persons for the delivery of money to a third person and for the release of the money to one of the first two persons upon the occurrence of some specified event. The arrangement is based on mutual distrust, the first two persons believing that in the absence of such an arrangement someone is likely to get "escrewed."

estop Verb, "to stop." Lawyers add the *e* in order to double the syllables and render the word meaningless to lay persons. It is on this linguistic theory that no lawyer in a restaurant will order "scargot." *See* escheat.

euthanasia a system of early retirement often urged on senior partners by the younger members of a law firm.

ex cathedra Latin, "from the chair." **1:** in canonical law, refers to any pronouncement based on papal authority.
2: in general, refers to any pronouncement issued without power of enforcement.

ex lax Latin, "from the lawyer." Refers to memos, briefs, and other work products of lawyers.

Federal Express an overnight delivery service that permits senior lawyers to assign twenty-four-hour projects to junior lawyers just thirty-six hours before the client needs the results. Federal Express vows *absolutely positively* to make timely delivery of urgent documents to the client's receptionist, security guard, mailroom, or other four-day holding service anywhere in the country.

fee **1:** in the law of real estate, full and unrestricted ownership of land.

2: a term whose loud utterance—"Fee?"—constitutes the lawyers' equivalent of "Is there a doctor in the house?"

fee tail **1:** In the law of real estate, a restricted form of ownership of land.

2: The oldest profession. (Not to be confused with "free tail"—*see* Club Med.)

fiduciary someone such as a bank trust officer or estate administrator on whom the law imposes a strict duty of loyalty and integrity. Usually a

FEE TAIL

lawyer, because other people maintain those qualities out of a sense of decency.

file cabinet   a five-drawer, manually activated trash compactor.

firm   an assemblage of lawyers. Similar to a "pride" of lions, "gaggle" of geese, "school" of sharks, or "bunch" of bananas, although sharks also frequently congregate in firms (as do a few bananas).

force majeure   in contract law, an irresistible force preventing the performance of your contractual obligations, such as a hurricane, flood, war, or the discovery that you could make a better profit elsewhere.

forum shopping   an attempt by a party in a lawsuit to obtain the home-court advantage. For example, someone with a Georgia accent would likely seek to avoid having his case tried in New York, where a jury might rule against him because they assumed he was stupid and bigoted. Similarly, someone with a New York accent would seek to avoid having his case tried in Georgia, where a jury might rule against him because they realized he was from New York.

Freedom of Information Act   a controversial law that permits citizens to examine official documents in the hands of the federal government. Exceptions to this rule include documents relating to an ongoing criminal investigation, documents that might jeopardize national security, documents whose exposure would impair the reelection prospects of the current administration, and documents whose assembly would require thought or exertion on the part of a federal bureaucrat.

Full Cleveland a professional outfit consisting of a dark blue button-down shirt, white polyester tie, white belt, and white patent-leather loafers. If you wear the Full Cleveland (or even variations thereof: the One-Third Cleveland or the Two-Thirds Cleveland), your firm may condemn you to its branch office there. (Warning: In Cleveland, this is known as the Full Pittsburgh.)

fully diluted **1:** a corporation's earnings restated to reflect the potential conversion of certain types of bonds or preferred stock into common shares.

2: by analogy to corporate earnings, a law firm's productive capacity (total document output divided by number of lawyers) restated to reflect the "contribution" of senior partners and brand-new associates (in other words, by increasing the denominator without changing the numerator).

3: a martini with more than three drops of vermouth.

garnishment the legal process by which your wages are channeled from your employer to your creditors in order to reduce your debts—and also to induce you to seek work elsewhere.

gift causa mortis Latin, "a gift caused by death." Refers to the legal doctrine that although most gifts are irrevocable (in contrast to the policy reportedly applied in Native American jurisdictions), a gift made in anticipation of your own death may be reclaimed if your death does not occur reasonably expeditiously.

golden parachute a fat, noncancelable, long-term employment contract designed to cushion the fall of executives who are bounced after a hostile takeover of their company. The most deft parachute stuffer to date, according to the *Guinness Book of World Records,* is ex–Bendix chief Bill "Ripcord" Agee, who in 1982 packed himself a whopping $4-million parachute. Moral: The bigger they are, the softer they fall.

good training a euphemism used in job interviews to describe those grim years you spent as an indentured servant in one of the megafirms of New York, Los Angeles, or some equally hospitable environment.

goodwill in the law of corporations, a catchall category located on the asset side of a company's balance sheet to make its assets appear to equal its liabilities. It includes valuable intangibles, such as a recognizable brand name or favorable publicity. For example, the arrest of John DeLorean did much to boost the goodwill of his DMC-12, the first car in history for which California collectors almost had license plates handmade by the company founder.

GSI *"Give-a-Shit Index."* A critical barometer by which young lawyers measure their continuing interest in big-firm practice. Ironically, the more you've had to eat, the less you're inclined to give.

habeas corpus Latin, "you've got a body." **1:** a judicial order directing an officer who has custody of a prisoner to come to court in order for the court to determine whether the prisoner is being illegally detained.

2: a conversation opener at discotheques in ancient Rome.

Hamburger Rule A direct if inelegant statement of the standard law-firm policy with respect to intrafirm dating: Don't get your meat where you get your bread. Also known as the Fountain Pen Rule: Don't dip yours in the company inkwell.

headhunter a legal body snatcher who makes a living by swelling heads, not shrinking them. Modern-day headhunters lure you from your current firm by painting visions of prestige, financial Valhalla, and "guaranteed partnership within two years." On the evolutionary scale, one step above private process server and one step below toaster oven.

health a technical term sometimes improperly

used to characterize the unfortunate plight of your client whose severe whiplash and other maladies are obvious to everyone but American-trained physicians.

holiday an occasion on which young lawyers are permitted to wear casual attire to the office.

homicide the expiration of one human being at the hands of another. The three basic categories of homicide are: felonious, forgivable, and praiseworthy, although victims rarely express a preference; the classification is for the lawyers.

hung jury a divided jury, i.e., one in which the jurors cannot reach agreement on the question of the defendant's guilt or innocence. Ironic term, because if the jury is hung, the defendant isn't. *Compare* well-hung jury.

id. abbreviation of "idem," Latin, meaning "the same." **1:** in legal writing, a reference to the immediately preceding authority.

2: in psychoanalytic theory, a repetition of a long-forgotten citation.

illegitimi non carborundum Latin, "don't let the bastards get you down." **1:** the motto of lawyers who deal with the IRS.

2: an expression of encouragement commonly offered by sensitive divorce lawyers to clients—e.g., King Arthur—whose illegitimate offspring threaten to complicate their affairs.

impeach **1:** with reference to a public official, to charge him with misconduct or incompetence.

2: with reference to a witness, to attempt to undermine his credibility, as by showing him to be a liar, drug addict, thespian, or Methodist.

3: in criminal law, to commit homicide by bombardment with the corrugated endocarps of fuzzy fruits.

in forma pauperis Latin, "in the form of a pau-

ID.

"No, I think my *id.* is under control. However,
I'm a little concerned about my *supra* and *infra.*"

IN FORMA PAUPERIS

per." A mode of proceeding in court whereby a litigant declares himself destitute in order to be excused from paying court filing fees and other expenses. A litigant's claim of poverty, whether accurate or not at the outset of the lawsuit, is usually incontestable following payment of his legal fees.

In God We Trust a legal principle indicating the only client for whom a lawyer will commence work without payment of a retainer.

in loco parentis **1:** Latin, "in the place of a parent." **2:** Spanish, "crazy momma."

inter alia Latin, "among other things." A term used by lawyers and judges to sound erudite when they cannot think of any other examples to support a given point.

interrogatory a written inquiry seeking information from an opposing party in a lawsuit. The difference between a "question" and an "interrogatory" is four syllables—hence lawyers' preference for the latter.

intestate **1:** one who dies without a will.
2: a glandular problem common among male lawyers, which isn't as painful as it sounds, although you shouldn't bring it up at cocktail parties.

IRS *I*nfernal *R*evenue *S*ervice.

J.D. Abbreviation of Latin, "*Juris Doctor*," meaning "Doctor of Laws." A *doctoral* degree given to *bachelor*-level students who have yet to *master* any substantive skills.

judge a unicameral legislative body.

judgment proof refers to someone against whom a judgment for damages would be meaningless, either because (1) he has no assets to collect, or (2) he is related to the sheriff.

judicial of or pertaining to a judge. (Entirely unrelated to the term "judicious.")

judicial clerk a recent law-school graduate who by virtue of high grades or personal contacts has secured the prestigious position of assistant to a judge. A judicial clerk's duties range from the menial (writing opinions, interpreting law, deciding cases) to the august (serving the judge lunch, helping the judge put on her robes, picking up the judge's laundry). In general, a judicial clerkship is a device by which a young lawyer postpones working for a living.

J.D.

"You didn't know I'm a Juris Doctor...? Oh, Angela, I thought the whole world knew that."

JUDGE

"Oyez, oyez, oyez. The Intermediate Superior
Court for the Western District of Upper Peninsula is
now in order, the Honorable E. Jefferson Farnsworth
presiding, larger than life."

jury a body of six to twelve individuals, usually retired or otherwise unemployed, hired by the state to sleep through talks by lawyers and judges before ruling in favor of whichever litigant's race, sex, and other circumstances most clearly resemble their own.

jury instructions instructions given by a judge to a jury prior to the jury's deliberations on a case. These instructions are followed about as closely as you followed the instructions that came with the Erector set or dollhouse you got when you were in the first grade.

juvenile court where teenage muggers, rapists, and arsonists go for someone to decide whether these high-spirited youngsters should lose their allowances for a week or whether less severe discipline will suffice.

KANGAROO COURT

lady lawyer an archaic term indicating a member of the legal profession who refers to venerable legal precedents not as "seminal" but as "ovular."

last clear chance **1:** in the law of torts, the doctrine that liability (as for an automobile collision) should rest with the person who had the last opportunity to avoid the collision.
2: for people who aspire to happiness in life, the moment before taking the LSATs.

lawyer someone trained in the manipulation of the law. For corporations, there are two distinct types of lawyers: "in-house" and "out-house," the latter term accurately suggesting the nature of what lawyers produce.

law review a law school magazine published four to eight times per year (except at Yale, which occasionally skips a year). Usually characterized by a footnote-to-text ratio of at least five to one, an eight- to twelve-month lag between the date designated on each issue and the date of release, and a two-inch layer of dust on bound

BRASWELL C.
COLEMAN, IIII.
~ ESQUIRE ~
DEFENDER OF
THE RICH
AND
OPPRESSIVE

LAWYER

LAW REVIEW

"If I had only known the influence Law Review carries with women, I would have studied harder first year."

LAWSUIT

"Every irascible coot in the country wants to sue somebody, thank God."

volumes in law-firm libraries (although this last point could change if the *Columbia Law Review* moves forward with its plan for a summer swimsuit issue).

laymen what lawyers call the people they screw.

Learned Hand **1:** a prominent twentieth-century judge on the United States Court of Appeals. **2:** a sixteenth-century court eunuch in Istanbul. (Not related to Learned Tongue.)

legal advice to the extent that "advice" implies counsel of an informal nature and without compensation to the lawyer, this term imbues with special meaning the notion of getting what you pay for. The lawyer is to be taken at his word when he offers uncompensated counsel accompanied by the statement, "This is the least I can do for you."

legalese an obscure language, based on Latin (and hopefully destined for the same fate), which lawyers use to prevent laymen from understanding what they're being charged with and for.

legal ethics a classic oxymoron, along the lines of "jumbo shrimp," "scholar athlete," "Amtrak schedule," "postal service," and "Justice Rehnquist."

legal pad **1:** yellow writing tablet. **2:** the residence of a hip lawyer. **3:** that extra something built into a lawyer's bill.

legal writing a bizarre branch of the something-from-nothing magical arts, rumored to have its origins in Oriental mysticism but also bearing a striking resemblance to a Middle Eastern loaves-

LEGAL ETHICS

"Of course ethics are important, son. But a law office is no place for fanaticism."

and-fishes trick first performed almost two centuries ago. Practitioners of this art are capable of miraculously expanding an implausible comment, such as "The sky is blue," into an elegantly persuasive declaration, such as "In some parts of the world, and possibly the universe, what is generally thought of as the sky (absent inclement weather) is likely, for a person of normal perceptive capacities (who is outside, looking up, during the daytime), to approximate that portion of the color spectrum currently designated 'blue.'"

legislative law a euphemism for an area of quasi-legal expertise more commonly known as lobbying. This term is employed by lawyers and defeated politicians who are too embarrassed to admit they make their living by mounting paid assaults on the public interest.

lex loci 1: Latin, "the law of the place." In the law of contracts, the rule that an agreement must be interpreted and enforced in accordance with the law of the place where it was made or to be performed.

2: Greek, "the law of locusts." An allusion to the Biblical prophecy that a person not bearing the seal of God on his forehead at the time of the Apocalypse will be subjected to five months of living hell by warriorlike locusts from the bottomless pit. (Revelations 9:3–11). Reference to this prophecy is standard in lawyers' billing statements to clients behind in their payments.

Lexis a machine that can do everything a young

lawyer can do, but without criticizing senior partners or demanding higher pay.

liar someone who habitually speaks untruths. The term is perilously close to "lawyer" and is viewed by many as synonymous with it. Hence the venerable joke:

Q: How can you tell when a lawyer is lying?
A: His lips are moving.

litigation in the American legal system, a basic right which guarantees every person his decade in court.

LSAT *Law School Aptitude Test.* An examination required for admission to law school and consisting of questions such as the following:

Directions: Read the following passage and blacken the space beside the answer you believe is most nearly correct.

"It was the best of times, it was the worst of times, it was the age of wisdom, it was the age of foolishness... [read the novel *A Tale of Two Cities,* attached to your exam booklet]... it is a far, far better rest that I go to than I have ever known."

Question: In the above story, what time is it?
☐ (a) The best of times.
☐ (b) The worst of times.
☐ (c) *The New York Times.*
☐ (d) About two o'clock.

LITIGATOR

"Mirror, mirror standing there,
who has Clarence Darrow's flair?"

malpractice failure to exercise reasonable care, and to possess a standard minimum of expertise, on the part of physicians, accountants, architects, engineers, and other professionals, except lawyers. Such failure on the part of lawyers is referred to as "unfortunate."

MBA *M*aster of *B*usiness *A*dministration. A degree lawyers wish they had so they could be issuing the orders rather than following them. As corporate lawyers know, these *M*aster *B*ull *A*rtists give special meaning to the phrase "often in error, but seldom in doubt."

mechanic's lien refers to the rule that someone who has done work for you but has not yet been paid has a top-priority claim on the structure on which the work was done. This is why it's important not to bounce a check to your dentist: Your fillings could be confiscated without notice or opportunity to floss. (Moral: Avoid a brush with the law.)

Melvin Belli **1:** A prominent U.S. trial lawyer. **2:** Latin, "Meet me in Bhopal."

memo to file a document on which lawyers record actions they wish they had taken or information they wish they had remembered to convey to the client.

mens rea Latin, "criminal mind." Refers to the level of mental culpability required for conviction of most crimes. For example, the difference between third-degree, second-degree, and first-degree murder is the difference between, respectively, "I had no idea she couldn't swim," "What did I care if she couldn't swim?" and "I should have tied chains to her feet."

Miranda rights named after Ernesto Miranda, a public-minded citizen who beat hell out of somebody in an Arizona bar in order to produce a test case regarding arrested persons' constitutional rights. Refers to your right as an American citizen to be informed upon being arrested that you may remain silent, that you are entitled to a lawyer, and that anything you say may be used against you in court. Your arresting officer is required to recite this information even if you are drunk, don't speak English, and seven members of the Moral Majority have just stomped you senseless because you don't love Jesus.

mislaid property property which has been deliberately left in a particular place and then forgotten. This is in contrast to "lost" property, which has been accidentally left nowhere in particular—

MIRANDA RIGHTS

"You have the right to remain silent . . ."

the sort of distinction that hallmarks a truly advanced jurisprudence.

misprision **1:** violation by a public official of any official duty.

2: a jail for women.

Monopoly a children's game popularized in the 1930s after the adult version was outlawed by the Sherman Antitrust Act of 1890. Under the auspices of the Republican Justice Department, the original version is regaining its popularity.

moot court a court whose rulings are of no practical significance. *See,* e.g., The Hague.

mother-in-law as distinguished from a mother-in-equity, someone with no discretion.

motion for enlargement **1:** a formal request that a court extend a deadline (or, in effect, "enlarge the time") for submission of a brief or other filing.

2: any of various exertions designed to promote personal pleasure and the preservation of the species. (Also known as "motion for extension.")

mushroom theory the tried-and-true theory by which large law firms develop the talents and skills of their new associates. The theory mandates three basic measures: Keep young lawyers in the dark, regularly dump manure on them, and can them as they approach maturity.

name partner with reference to a large law firm, refers to the imaginative, entrepreneurial, independent-minded and now deceased lawyers who gave their names to the institution they founded—and who would never have stepped foot in a place like what it has become.

negligence a failure to exercise reasonable prudence, with resulting harm to someone else. The universality of the right to reasonably prudent care by one's neighbors is illustrated in *Robinson v. Pioche, Bayerque & Co.* (California 1885): "A drunken man is as much entitled to a safe street as a sober one, and much more in need of it."

net lease in real estate leasing, a rental agreement under which the maintenance, utilities, taxes, and insurance are to be paid by the tenant.

net net lease in real estate leasing, the same thing as a net lease, but this time they mean it.

net net net lease in real estate leasing, the same thing as a net net lease, but this time they mean

NET NET NET LEASE

"I *expected* to pay for utilities, Mr. Snead, and I'm *willing* to pay for plumbing repairs. But I'll be damned if I'm going to pay for your son's college tuition."

it, and the tenant also pays the landlord's alimony.

nonequity partner in a law firm, someone who looks, sounds, works, and is compensated like an associate. In fact, someone who *is* an associate.

nonpaying client someone soon to be in need of a new lawyer.

not guilty a jury verdict reflecting: (1) in rare instances, a lack of guilt; (2) most of the time, uncertainty as to guilt; (3) always, suppressed evidence of guilt.

nudum pactum Latin, "naked contract." Any of various international accords involving third-world leaders whose willingness to refrain from smuggling zipguns, bicycle chains, and scimitars into negotiating sessions can be confirmed only by conducting the sessions buck naked.

nuisance the tort of interfering with a person's use or enjoyment of his property. For example, in your condominium complex, your obnoxious upstairs neighbor who insists on playing loud abrasive music at times when decent people like you are trying to sleep, not to mention your swinish downstairs neighbor, the insomniac, who bangs on his ceiling with a broomstick at all hours of the night because he's too much of a philistine to appreciate the tasteful melodies (and other rhythmic sounds) that occasionally waft out of your pad at 4:00 A.M.

NUDUM PACTUM

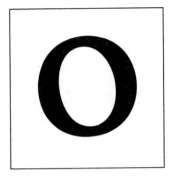

obiter dictum Latin, "saying by the way." Refers to gratuitous words in judicial opinions, particularly those added by judges to the drafts of their clerks.

objection the cry of a lawyer who sees truth about to creep into the courtroom.

obscenity refers to books, pictures, and movies of a prurient nature and without socially redeeming value except to the overcoat-in-the-back-row crew. Often difficult to identify, except by former Justice Potter Stewart, who by his own claim knew it when he saw it.

of counsel an ad-hoc contractual arrangement between a law firm and any lawyer whose worth the firm suspects may be beneath that of its lowest-paid partner. Often the semiretired status of an elderly but still well-connected lawyer whom the firm compassionately refrains from throwing out on the street for fear that major clients will do the same to the firm.

one-bite rule in the law of torts, the doctrine that

a domestic animal (e.g., your eighty-seven-pound Doberman) is not deemed to have "known vicious propensities," and hence you as the owner are not considered negligent for failing to keep it tied up—until it has bitten someone at least once. Moral: You and your Doberman get one free bite. Make it count.

One L **1:** at Harvard, a first-year law student, as opposed to a Two L (second-year law student), Three L (third-year law student), Pre-L (undergraduate with no chance of getting into medical school), or No-L (a seasonal reference in Christian mythology).

2: at Yale, a mnemonic device to assist students in spelling the name of their school.

opinion letter a document consisting of one page of legal advice and nine pages of disclaimers, caveats, limitations, qualifications, and refusals to take responsibility for whatever that crazy client might do next.

Order of the Coif a legal fraternity composed of balding law students and dedicated to the revival of noncontemporary head-wear. At some schools, also known as "Order of the Sombrero" and "Order of the Pith Helmet."

OSHA **1:** *O*ccupational *S*afety and *H*ealth *A*dministration.

2: a polite contraction of "oh, shit," the usual response of legal associates upon being assigned a research project involving regulations of the Occupational Safety and Health Administration.

oyez Anglo-French, "hear ye." A cry issued three

ONE-BITE RULE

"The Court finds for the defendant, Fido MacGregor."

times before commencement of proceedings of the Supreme Court, even if the room is empty. No one knows why. Similar to Yiddish, "Oy, oy, oy."

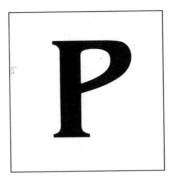

palimony wages of sin.

par **1:** the nominal value, such as one dollar, assigned to a share of stock.

2: any *acceptably* good performance; in golf, for example, a score of one stroke per round higher than your biggest client.

parachuter someone who enters a law firm laterally—i.e., after working somewhere else—rather than coming in straight from law school. Invariably loathed by those beneath him in seniority.

paralegal a legal secretary who can't type.

parole a conditional release from prison for the purpose of allowing the parolee to demonstrate the inadequacy of the original sentence.

partner a usually senior member of a law firm whose compensation consists of a percentage of firm profits rather than a fixed salary and who has a vote in the firm's decisions. Commonly identifiable by any of the following: gray hair, no hair, coronary condition, Mercedes. Within a

PARTNER

''Step to it, Skelly . . . if my train drags, it's your ass.''

law firm, the term denotes a professional relationship—not affection.

per curiam Latin, "None of us wants to take the blame."

per stirpes Latin, "by the root." **1:** in the law of wills, a rule providing for the distribution of a deceased's property equally among a given class of descendants.

2: any inheritance which passes equally to all virally diseased offspring.

photocopier **1:** a device that shreds the originals of documents bearing client signatures.

2: a treasured office fringe benefit, especially for givers of large parties, would-be novelists, and people who get their ya-yas making flat-fleshed portraits of parts of their anatomy.

physician **1:** the ideal client.

2: the ideal defendant. *Compare* Fort Knox.

pinstripe the *de rigueur* staple of legal fashion, reflecting the venerable maxim, "Think Yiddish, dress British." (Note: The stripes of your suits should generally be narrower than those worn by your former clients now residing at San Quentin.)

pole attachment **1:** in communications law, the affixing of cable television wires to telephone and electric utility poles, a practice that raises issues involving which of the utilities' expenses may be charged to the cable franchises. Practitioners in this area spend much of their time calculating the costs of the erection of bare poles

PINSTRIPE

"Love the suit, Henderson. Love the suit."

installed, although some become too aroused by such concepts to calculate anything.

2: in Warsaw, incarceration of labor dissidents.

pornography any film or printed material so sexually explicit that a judge gets to look at it behind locked doors before deciding whether it is suitable for public consumption.

police brutality the use of force by police against persons of your own race, creed, or political persuasion.

prayer for relief **1:** the clause in a complaint that describes the nature of the relief sought.

2: an especially urgent demand for fee tail. *Compare* common pleas.

prison where clients go when lawyers screw up.

> CLIENT (upon hearing guilty verdict): "Where do we go now?"
> LAWYER (closing briefcase): "*I'm* going back to my office."

private placement an offering of stock for which no registration with state or federal securities authorities is required. Not to be confused with a "privates placement"—the syndication of a thoroughbred racehorse's stud rights.

probate the often interminable process of determining in court the authenticity and validity of a will. Bequeathing millions of dollars to a university to have a building named in your honor may preserve your memory for a while, but he who would truly be remembered and discussed

PORNOGRAPHY

PRAYER FOR RELIEF

"Forgive me, Father, for I have obfuscated."

for centuries will leave behind two or more inconsistent and undated wills.

pro bono publico Latin, "for the public good." Refers to legal services performed without charge, usually for ingrates.

productivity bonus a once-a-year bonus that many law firms pay associates who have gone above and beyond the normal call of workaholism. The level of your productivity bonus, if any, can be calculated by the following Wall Street formula:

$$\left[\frac{(H_1 + (H_2)^N)}{S} - \frac{(R+E)}{} \times \frac{(B+V)^2}{} + \frac{Q}{O}\right]^W \times C$$

Productivity Bonus formula:

B = Size of your briefcase
C = Your chances of finding work elsewhere
E = Exercise time
H_1 = Hours worked
H_2 = Additional hours that may be billed to clients by double billing or other multiplier techniques
N = Number of clients to whom H_2-type units of time may be billed
Q = Quality of work
R = Rest room time
S = Sleep
V = Number of vests you own
W = Whom you work for

profit 1: the difference between a law firm's expenses and its revenues.

2: the bottom line.

3: the meaning of life.

pro se Latin, "for yourself." Refers to the lawful but inadvisable act of representing yourself in court. Even lawyers hire other lawyers to represent them in court, so embarrassing is it to utter outrageous alibis on your own behalf.

public defender an ironic term for a defense lawyer who at public expense endeavors to free known felons for further assaults on the public.

public interest law firm a misnomer for a private law firm whose cases are selected with an eye to achieving social goals that a narrow segment of the public believes to be in the rest of the public's interest.

quack in medical malpractice cases, the physician who testifies for your opponent.

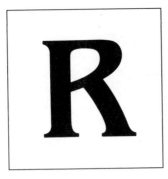

rainmaker   a lawyer whose compensation bears no relation to his legal skills. Usually an indispensable grayhair who brings business in the door but doesn't have the faintest idea of what to do with it once it's there.

ratio decidendi   **1:** Latin, "the reason for the decision." The reasons articulated in a judge's opinion for why she ruled the way she did. This may on occasion coincide with why she actually ruled the way she did.

2: Greek, "ratio of decision." A critical financial ratio, consisting of the percentage of company stock owned by its founder, divided by the total stock outstanding. Useful for determining whether to marry into the founder's family.

real estate   as distingiushed from *un*real estate, refers to two categories of things: (1) land, earth, soil, dirt—everything along these lines except what your potted plant is sitting in and what accumulates between your toes after you've been wearing sandals awhile; and (2) "fixtures"— build-

RAINMAKER

"I know, it's crazy, but last year he brought in two huge clients."

ings, and other structures so large, heavy, and immobile as to be virtually part of the land. This category includes Caucasian basketball players and most blind dates.

recruiting lunch a meal, invariably expensive, by which law-firm recruiters misleadingly attempt to demonstrate to prospective lawyers the kind of life-style they would have the money to enjoy if they became associates at the firm—and the *time* to enjoy upon retiring from the practice of law.

recusal the process by which a judge disqualifies himself from a case because he has an apparent stake in the result. Recusal is often voluntary, unless the judge has a *real* stake in the result.

red-eye an occupational hazard of a bicoastal law practice which demands that you take overnight planes from the west coast to the east coast in order to arrive at the office early enough to nap at your desk all day.

regulation an unreadable sentence, having the force of law, promulgated by bureaucrats at the FDA, FAA, FHA, FTC, FCC, or other F-ing federal agencies.

res ipsa loquitur 1: An evidentiary rule stated in Latin, meaning "The thing (*res*) speaks (*loquitur*) for itself (*ipsa*)." Note that the words are out of order. No wonder Latin is a dead language.
2: Greek, "It won't stop talking." A legal defense to the crime of killing parrots and myna birds.

respondeat superior 1: Latin, "Let the master respond." In the law of torts, refers to the rule that an employer may in some circumstances be liable for the wrongful acts of his employees.

2: Greek, "Let the one on top respond." Refers to the old common-law rule (now enforced only in Maine) that whoever holds the topmost position in intimate conjugal circumstances is required to handle interruptions by the telephone or door bell.

responsibility something for which young lawyers universally clamor—until they get it.

rule against perpetuities any of various rules designed to deal with senior partners who won't work or retire. More honored in the breach than the observance.

SEC *S*ecurities and *E*xchange *C*ommission, a federal agency devoted to providing young lawyers with the experience necessary to secure jobs advising corporations on how to circumvent the regulations of the SEC.

secretary the power behind the phone. An overworked, underpaid, notoriously unhappy member of the legal proletariat, whose work for junior lawyers consists of reading *Cosmopolitan* or *GQ*, and for senior lawyers, screening out United Way fund raisers.

security a term that for lawyers denotes technical specifications pertaining to stocks and bonds, but that for normal people represents a verbal Rorschach test. Test yourself: What first comes to mind when you hear the word *security*? (1) Blanket, (2) Chain lock, (3) Malpractice insurance, (4) The roll bar on your convertible, (5) A comfort letter from Sullivan & Cromwell.

self-help a common-law alternative to fee tail. *See* unclean hands.

service of process the presenting or "serving" of

notice of a lawsuit to the person being sued. Service of process is performed either by government marshals or by private contractors, the latter consisting primarily of former bar bouncers and professional mud wrestlers, many bearing a striking resemblance to Mr. T.

settlement a device by which lawyers obtain fees without working for them.

sex a recreational activity capable of being performed by groups of any number, including, as lawyers all too frequently demonstrate, one.

shark repellent any of various measures a company's management might take to make the company appear less attractive to hostile acquirers—for example, purchasing another company similar to the acquirer so as to produce antitrust problems; carrying out a scorched-earth policy, as by selling off the company's most valuable assets and trashing the executive washroom; or electing Jane Fonda or Mary Cunningham to the board of directors.

s/he pronounced *she-he*. A new pronoun invented by lawyers to reduce a company's vulnerability to sex discrimination suits because of bias in job descriptions ("The applicant must be able to type 60 wpm, and s/he must also have great legs").

small claims court a "small change court" shunned by lawyers because the stakes are limited and because there is nothing to be had there but justice.

smell test the most stringent of five tests for determining the permissibility of uttering im-

SERVICE OF PROCESS

"The pleasure of your company is expected in court, madam...gratuity not included."

plausible statements on behalf of your client in court. Some arguments just plain smell bad—and may even have people in the courtroom checking the bottoms of their shoes. The other four tests, in descending order of stringency, are: The "blush" test—can you make the argument without turning visibly red? The "straight face" test—can you finish your entire sentence without starting to laugh? The "barf" test—will propounding your client's alibi cause you to gag from the outrageousness of your own words? And the "wrath of God" test—is the theory so unsupportable that its very utterance may cause lightning to strike even as you speak?

Socratic method a law-school teaching method, also known as "learning through humiliation," that involves a dialogue between a law professor and a randomly chosen student, the dialogue continuing until the latter yields either the proper answer, tears, or vomit. For example:

PROFESSOR YUDKOWITZ: Ms. Robertson, what thought is currently passing through my mind?

STUDENT ROBERTSON: Excuse me?

PROFESSOR YUDKOWITZ: Perhaps your mother will excuse you. I will not. Did you read today's assignment?

STUDENT ROBERTSON: Yes...absolutely...but...

PROFESSOR YUDKOWITZ: Then why aren't you able to answer a simple question?

STUDENT ROBERTSON: I...I don't know.

PROFESSOR YUDKOWITZ: I regret to say that your future in the law appears bleak.

SMELL TEST

"Attridge, at this firm there's *nothing* that can't pass the smell test."

SOCRATIC METHOD

"No wonder Socrates killed himself."

squawk box a two-way desktop telephone speaker. This is a classic "power accessory," enabling its owner to implicitly communicate one or more of the following "power messages" to the person at the other end of the line: (1) I'm too busy to free up even one hand; (2) You aren't important enough to warrant my lifting the receiver; or (3) My secretary and I are up to something you'd love to get in on.

standing something you're required to have in order to maintain a lawsuit. In general, refers to a concrete personal interest, as opposed to a purely academic interest, in obtaining the relief demanded. For example, when you've been run over by a cement mixer, your broken legs give you standing.

stare decisis **1:** Latin, "to stand by what has been decided." The judicial habit of citing precedents that coincide with how the judge wishes to rule. **2:** Greek, "to stare decisively." In criminal law, the process by which an assault victim indicates which of the suspects in a lineup he believes to have been his assailant.

statutory rape the crime of sexual intercourse with someone whom the law presumes to be too young to be capable of giving meaningful consent to so intimate an act. *Compare* Statutory French Kissing, 17 Texas Code S. 39.01(b). Reformers have criticized the gender bias inherent in most statutory rape provisions, whose phraseology reflects a belief that when a man has sex with a young girl, it's rape, whereas when a woman has sex with a young boy, she's doing him a favor.

subornation of perjury **1:** inducing a witness to lie while under oath.

  2: a technical term that nitpicking lawyers for the other side apply to the routine process that you call "preparing the witness."

suffrage **1:** the right to vote.

  2: what you experience at a cocktail party where the lawyer-to-layman ratio exceeds one-to-ten.

sui generis **1:** Latin, "of its own kind." A term commonly used by lawyers to stress the special circumstances that led their clients to commit the crimes for which they're being tried.

  2: Greek, "a charitable hog."

summary judgment a dispositive judicial ruling. The term "summary" is ironic, in that it suggests that *other* rulings by a judge are the product of deliberation and care.

summer clerk an overpaid, underabused, prospective grunt vacationing at a private law firm between years of law school.

Supreme Court the place where the finest legal minds in the country gather—to serve as law clerks to the Justices.

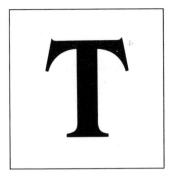

taxes of life's two certainties, the only one for which you can get an automatic extension.

tenancy by the entirety 1: in the law of real property, a form of joint ownership of land by a husband and wife.

2: Siamese twins.

10-K the form on which corporations file their annual financial reports with the SEC. Not to be confused with a 10-k, which is a 6.2-mile roadrace, or $10K, which is the least you'll ever pay to have a lawyer prepare your 10-K.

tort anything for which you can sue someone—e.g., stabbing you, libeling you, setting you up with blind dates whose horizontal dimensions exceed their vertical—other than breach of contract (which is called, coincidentally, breach of contract).

trespass quare clausum fregit Latin, "trespass wherefore he broke the close." Refers to a lawsuit in which the defendant is called upon to explain why he broke the plaintiff's "close," the real or imaginary structure enclosing the plaintiff's land. Not to be confused with *trespass quare Clause fregit,* which refers to a trespass onto a domestic rooftop on Christmas Eve.

TRO *T*emporary *R*estraining *O*rder. **1:** an emergency order of limited duration issuable by a judge at the request of only one party in a dispute. (Not to be confused with SRO, BSO, HBO, or SOB, the last being frequently employed by the lawyers for the other side to characterize the judge who granted the TRO.)
2: any of the all-too-common orders by which lawyers repel the inexplicably amorous advances of their spouses (e.g., "Not tonight, dear, I have a trust indenture").

trust a device by which the "legal" and "beneficial" ownership of property are separated, as where a "donor" (say, your grandfather) places a "corpus" (the family fortune) under the legal control of a "trustee" (a bank) to be managed for a "beneficiary" (you). The term "trust" is ironic: If your grandfather had any trust in you, you might now have control of the family fortune.

truss a device, similar to a trust, for conserving and maintaining the assets of the beneficiary.

unclean hands **1:** an equitable principle that no one may sue someone whom he has defrauded. Unrelated to the venerable criminal-law concept of "coming clean."
2: the likely consequence of the common-law remedy of self-help (*see*).

under advisement a place where judges hold cases indefinitely pending settlement by the parties.

union lawyer a lawyer who specializes in representing labor unions. Usually someone knowledgeable in the area of labor law who hasn't been able to acquire corporate clients.

unjust enrichment **1:** a last-ditch, throw-in-the-kitchen-sink, why-not-we've-tried-everything-else claim in a lawsuit against someone who has made out better in a deal than you have.
2: the compensation of first-year associates in big-city law firms.

usufruct **1:** in the law of real property, the right to enjoy the fruits of land owned by someone else.
2: an Italian gesture of contempt.

UNDER ADVISEMENT

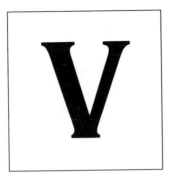

vacation among lawyers, a frequently discussed, little utilized period of varying duration (usually a weekend—in extreme instances, a weekend beginning at noon on Friday) in advance of which you drive yourself to exhaustion trying to clear your desk, and during which you lose sleep trying to remember what it was you forgot to take care of and dreading the pileup of work you'll encounter upon your return. Usually a source of relief when it's over.

vagrancy the crime of being a bum in public, especially if you smell bad, unless you're a jogger. In many jurisdictions vagrancy statutes have been declared unconstitutional because of their inherent vagueness and the inability of legislators to describe with sufficient precision the conduct they're trying to get at. Statutes that spoke in terms of being an able-bodied adult who refused to work for a living were construed as reaching U.S. senators. Statutes that spoke in terms of being "without visible means of support"

VACATION

were construed as reaching bra-burning feminists and occasional male athletes before the advent of Cruex.

verdict a device by which jurors are allowed, and even encouraged, to elevate common sense over the technicalities of the law. Often bears no relation to the evidence, thus demonstrating what the lawyers knew all along—the jurors weren't just concentrating with their eyes closed when that old coot in the black bathrobe was explaining what the case was all about.

vice any form of recreation, such as prostitution or gambling, so suspect that it must be investigated, analyzed, and even personally tested by legislators before it may be legalized.

voir dire French, "to speak the truth." The process by which lawyers question and weed out prospective jurors suspected of impartiality.

warranty a promise that goods being sold are truly as they appear to be. In particular, a promise for which the law will impose liability if it is not "strictly" true—in contrast to a "representation," which need only be "substantially" true. Thus, a car which is "warranted" to be operable must have four tires; a car which is merely "represented" to be operable need have only three. A warranty may be "express" or "implied," "exclusive" or "nonexclusive," and in New Jersey, "serious" or "just kidding."

watered stock **1:** in securities law, a stock issued for an amount less than its par value.
2: bloated cattle.

weekend the last two workdays in an associate's week.

white-collar crime **1:** Any of various nonviolent crimes, such as embezzlement or securities fraud, committed by Ivy Leaguers and other God-fearing pillars of society who consider holding people up at knife point to be at best quaint, at worst indecorous, and in any event small potatoes. **2:** the removal of buttons, placement of indelible stains, and a laundry list of other equally nefarious offenses committed against your dress shirts or blouses by commercial laundries. Invariably discovered five minutes or less before job interviews, board meetings, and press conferences.

will something that lets you wait until you're out of harm's way before revealing what you really thought of your spouse and children.

witness someone who testifies in court. Lawyers refer to witnesses as either "friendly" or "hostile," the latter usually suffering from an irritating proclivity to truthfulness.

word processor a machine for the mysterious deletion of words, sentences, and whole paragraphs from legal briefs the night before they're due in court.

WILL

"To my one true-blue ever-faithful companion..."

WITNESS

"Counsel will henceforth refrain from badgering the witness."

WORD PROCESSOR

"What the hell did you do with my brief?"

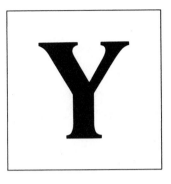

yellow dog contract in labor law, a now illegal form of contract by which an employer requires an employee to promise not to join a labor union. The term derives from the fact that the first such contract was between Old Yeller, who was then desperate for work (having been type-cast by Hollywood producers in what film professionals refer to as "dog" roles), and Walt Disney, an avuncular-looking man who was in fact shrewd enough to perceive in Old Yeller's plight an opportunity to avoid the superstar rates then being demanded by the likes of Lassie and Rin-Tin-Tin.

Yiddish the international language of negotiation. Occasionally used to insult your opponent, as in *gonif* (thief), *meshugener* (crazy), and the ultimate insult, *goyische* (a poor negotiator). More commonly, Yiddish words are used as terms of respect for your opponent, as in *maven* (expert), *makher* (a big wheel), and *gonif* (thief).

YELLOW DOG CONTRACT

"We can live without the fire hydrant provision, Mr. Hayes, but the time off during mating season is not negotiable."

zeal a level of earnestness and desire with which lawyers are exhorted by their Code of Professional Responsibility to represent clients. With respect to clients who pay their bills, this exhortation has proved gratuitous; with respect to nonpaying clients, futile.

zzz's the last word in legal research and writing.

ABOUT THE AUTHOR

D. Robert White is an attorney in Washington, D.C., and a frequent lecturer at law schools and bar conventions across the country. A native of Atlanta, Georgia, Mr. White graduated from Harvard College in 1975 and from Columbia Law School in 1979, where he was an articles editor of the *Columbia Law Review*. A former federal judicial clerk, Mr. White has succumbed to performing commercial litigation and general corporate work. His previous publications include: *The Official Lawyer's Handbook* (1983); "Pacifica Foundation v. FCC: 'Filthy Words,' the First Amendment, and the Broadcast Media," 78 *Colum. L. Rev.* 164 (1978); and the class history for the *Westminster Lynx,* his high school annual (1971).